Original title:
Sailing into the Sunset

Copyright © 2025 Creative Arts Management OÜ
All rights reserved.

Author: Amelia Montgomery
ISBN HARDBACK: 978-1-80581-574-7
ISBN PAPERBACK: 978-1-80581-101-5
ISBN EBOOK: 978-1-80581-574-7

Mist and Memory at Day's End

The sun dips low in a cartoon style,
As seagulls argue, all in a pile.
The captain slips, with a clumsy splash,
Yelling, 'Who's steering? I just had a flash!'

With sails so bright, like a circus tent,
Balloons are flying, our money well spent.
But now the wind has changed its scheme,
And we've lost half the crew to ice cream!

Odes to the Vanishing Light

The sky's ablaze, but who stole the shades?
Our navigation's lost; is that why it fades?
The lighthouse winks, playing hide-and-seek,
While pirates feast on last night's critique.

The dolphins dance, doing cha-cha-flips,
'We'll take the helm!' they say, as they grip.
But all we want is a cozy chair,
And some popcorn, with not a care!

A Voyage Beyond the Horizon

Off we go, in a boat that's too small,
We dream of glory, yet fear the fall.
The compass spins like it's on a spree,
'Is that the North Pole? Or just a tree?'

With pizza on deck, it's a floating feast,
But the fish are laughing, at least not the least.
'Is this a cruise or a carnival ride?'
As waves crash gently, and seagulls slide!

The Last Light at Sea

As dusk rolls in, we toast with our mugs,
Our ship's a friend, it's filled with shrugs.
The stars peek out, but where's the moon?
Is it hiding out, with a cosmic tune?

The captain sings "Yo-ho!" in the night,
While the crew debates if the stars are bright.
One says 'Twinkle; another sees a flare,'
And thus we drift, without a care!

Embracing the Dusk with Open Sails

The boat wobbles, a dance on waves,
The captain spills juice, it's how it braves.
Seagulls laugh at our clumsy route,
While we cheer, our hair's a hoot!

Stars peek out, what a grand view,
The fish are laughing, they join in too.
Our map is soggy, our snacks all gone,
Yet on we float, from dusk until dawn!

The Horizon's Gentle Caress

The sky's a canvas, all painted bright,
With colors that giggle, pure delight.
The breeze carries whispers, full of jest,
While we try figuring out which way's west.

A crab joins, he wants our chips,
With snapping claws, he takes quick quips.
Though we forgot sunscreen, oh what a sight,
We're glowing like lobsters, what a night!

Where Dreamers Meet the Tide

Dreamers gather, with hats askew,
While waves crash softly, as if they knew.
One claims to spot a mermaid's tail,
But it's just his shoe caught in the sail.

The tide pulls laughter, our spirits rise,
As jellyfish dodge our curious eyes.
We toast with sodas, a sugary cheer,
What a wild ride, to be stranded here!

The Melody of Dusk

A ukulele strums under fading light,
As dolphins dance, oh what a sight!
We sing like seagulls with silly tunes,
Chasing each other like playful loons.

With popcorn clouds drizzling pizza dreams,
We navigate on these whimsical beams.
The moon winks down, a sparkling friend,
Sailing laughs, until the journey's end!

Radiance on the Horizon's Edge

The boat made of rubber, it squeaks on the sea,
A seagull named Larry sings off-key for free.
The captain's a parrot, it squawks with delight,
Navigating waves while he sips on a Sprite.

The sky sets ablaze with hues of bright peach,
We laugh at our shadows that dance on the beach.
The fish tell us jokes as they bubble on by,
We giggle, we wiggle, under orange-pink sky.

Driftwood Dreams at Day's End

Driftwood collects all the fun of the day,
Each piece holds a story, in its own funny way.
We built a fine castle, it fell with a splat,
And now we're just stuck with a moldy old hat.

The tide rolls in gently, a ticklish tease,
We're splashed by the waves, and we're dodging the breeze.
The sunset's a party, a bright colored cake,
And who needs a fork when you have a good shake?

The Canvas of the Dimming Sky

As brushes of tangerine dip into the blue,
The giggles of jellyfish bubble, who knew?
We painted our boat with a rainbow of cheer,
Who knew crusty old barnacles could shed a tear?

The clouds are our canvas, they float and they sway,
We ramble on stories, till night steals the day.
Each star is a twinkle that winks at our plight,
We laugh till we're dizzy, ushering night.

Echoes of the Fading Sun

The waves whisper secrets that tickle our toes,
The sun rolls away with a giggle, it goes.
We slide off our boat with loud splashes and grins,
While crabs join the party, with twirls and with spins.

The echoes of laughter ring out from the shore,
While shadows are growing and tipsy, we soar.
As daylight takes flight, we chase after fun,
In search of new antics 'til everything's done.

The Vessel of Dreams Drifting

On a boat made of marshmallows,
We floated down candy streams.
Chasing jellyfish on rainbows,
With gumball fish in our dreams.

Our captain wore a giant hat,
With sunglasses perched on his nose.
He said, "Sail with me, it's a splat!"
As licorice winds began to blow.

The compass spun like a top,
While dolphins did the hula dance.
With every wave, we'd laugh and hop,
In our sugary, wobbly prance.

But as the sun began to wink,
We packed our snacks and waved goodbye.
With fudge as sails, and hearts in sync,
We sailed back home toward the sky.

Navigating the Crimson Tides

Upon the sea of strawberry jam,
We steered with jellybean cheer.
Our snacks afloat, what a grand slam,
As we devoured each wild sphere.

The seagulls squawked in disbelief,
As we toasted with our fruit punch.
"We're pirates now!" said Captain Leaf,
With a swig and a boisterous munch.

The waves were sticky, the sails were sweet,
With licorice ropes holding tight.
We danced to the rhythm of gumdrops' beat,
Under the candy-colored light.

As twilight fell with a giggle and grin,
We knew that our time was up.
But oh, the sugar rush we were in,
As we sailed back with our cup.

In the Wake of Day's End

In a boat made of pizza crust,
We coasted on a sea of cheese.
The nighttime stars began to adjust,
As we searched for tomato breeze.

Our crew was made of playful cats,
That wore tiny pirate hats.
They brought their own set of snacks,
As we laughed and played like brats.

"Ahoy!" we shouted at the moon,
As the olives danced on the waves.
We sang a silly, silly tune,
For all the snacks that we could save.

When the day turned spicy and dark,
We lit our lanterns with a flare.
Floating home with our pizza ark,
With laughter drifting in the air.

Driftwood and Dusk

On pieces of driftwood we skate,
Across seas of shimmering cream.
With sprinkling stars, we celebrate,
Each wave flows like a whipped dream.

The wind told jokes of yore,
As the sails flapped like eager hens.
We giggled until we could no more,
While kites made of toast held the pens.

Marshmallow clouds joined our high fun,
As we searched for a sweet surprise.
What treasure awaits 'neath the setting sun?
Perhaps something sticky and wise.

As the twilight kissed our boat's bow,
We danced with shadows of the night.
And driftwood dreams showed us just how,
To laugh until the morning light.

The Brilliance of Dusk's Call

The sky wears orange, what a sight,
My boat's a banana, feeling quite light.
The seagulls squawk like they won the race,
While I throw snacks in the water's embrace.

The waves seem to giggle, what cheeky pals,
They splash my shoes like mischievous gals.
A fish flipped by with a wink and a grin,
As if saying, "Hey, why not join in?"

A crab on the shore gives a playful cheer,
I join in the laughter, forgetting my fear.
My boat does a wiggle, it's quite a show,
Dusk's brilliance sparkles on my toe!

Cadences of the Setting Sun

On my tiny raft with snacks galore,
I might just drift off to nevermore.
The sun is a DJ, spinning bright tunes,
While I practice my dance with the clumsy loons.

The waves clap their hands, oh what fun!
My hat flies away — it's a marathon run!
A dolphin jumps high, does a flip in the air,
I cheer like a kid, full of joy and flair.

Stars peek out, whispering secrets so bold,
I wave back at them, "Just wait, I'm not old!"
In this symphony, life's a silly twist,
Dusk's playful tunes, hard to resist!

A Harbor in the Glow

In this brightness, the water's a mirror,
My boat is a party, with no hint of fear.
The sunset's a chef, cooking dishes of gold,
While I munch on chips, being carefree and bold.

A tugboat honks loud, it's got jokes to tell,
"Why did the sailor think he'd do well?"
"Because he had a buoyant sense of humor!"
Laughter erupts, it feels like a tumor!

I wave at the sunset, my old pal indeed,
"Don't let the clouds win, let's take the lead!"
As night falls, I turn my boat around,
A harbor in glow, it's joy that I've found!

Twilight's Edge

Twilight's here, with its funny little quirks,
My friends are all fishes, with goofy smirks.
The horizon's blushing, a colorful child,
And I'm just a sailor, a bit wild and mild.

The wind plays tricks, it gives me a shove,
I hope it's not angry, I sent it my love.
A pelican swoops down, trying to steal,
My last bit of sandwich — what a raw deal!

But I laugh it off, good vibes in the air,
With twilight's brushstrokes, nothing can compare.
As stars prance above, I try to keep track,
In this wacky world, there's no looking back!

Echoes of Golden Reflections

A pirate parrot on the deck,
Squawking tales of gold and speck.
The captain's hat flies off with glee,
Chasing it, the crew sips tea.

The map unfolds, but wait, oh no!
It's a treasure hunt for taco dough.
With every wave, we roll and laugh,
Paddle on, we're a funny craft!

Mermaids peek with curious eyes,
Dancing wildly 'neath the skies.
We toss them chips, they toss us seas,
Our joy afloat, on salty breeze.

As day retreats and night draws near,
We sing our shanties full of cheer.
With pots of gold all turning blue,
Our sunset fun is just for two!

Tranquil Journeys at Dusk

The boat's a squeaky merry-go,
With rubber ducks lined in a row.
We wave goodbye to the day's bright rays,
And bid adieu to serious ways.

A jellyfish floats, wearing a crown,
While seagulls giggle, diving down.
We pretend to catch each splashy wave,
Acting bold, though none are brave.

The sun spills colors, orange and pink,
As fish attempt to grasp a wink.
"Did you see that one jump so high?"
"No, I'm busy with my pie!"

Our laughter echoes through the night,
With sandwiches flying left and right.
In this soft glow, we dance and sway,
On tranquil journeys, we've lost our way!

A Realm of Crimson Waters

The sky's on fire, or so it seems,
As we set sail with huge ice creams.
A showdown with a dolphin fleet,
Who steals our snacks with lightning feet!

The waves are giggling with delight,
A surfboard's wedged in a starry light.
As fish throw parties, we join in fun,
Dancing 'round like we've just won!

A pirate's map leads us astray,
To an island of socks where mermaids play.
With spinning shells, they sing a tune,
"Trying to catch us? Better bring a broom!"

Crimson hues wrap every wave,
As we escape, it's laughter we crave.
In this realm where chaos spins,
We're all just fools who wear big grins!

Setting Foot on Starlit Waves

With sandals on, we trip and flop,
As jellyfish join our hopping bop.
The stars above give us a wink,
Sipping juice from a dotted pink.

An octopus plays a trumpet loud,
As we attempt to gather a crowd.
With every note, we twist and turn,
Paddle past and feel the burn!

Splat on deck, a seagull's aim,
We laugh so hard, we lose the game.
Caught between giggles and funny scenes,
Sharing secrets with the fishy queens.

As waves embrace our crazy ride,
We dance with joy, our hearts wide.
In the starlit glow, we make our cheers,
To funny tales that last for years!

The Horizon's Embrace

We set forth on a boat so grand,
With seagulls arguing, a silly band.
The captain's hat flew, much to our glee,
As we rocked and rolled, just like the sea.

The fish waved hello, they thought it was neat,
As we danced on deck, our moves quite a feat.
I tripped on a rope, oh what a surprise,
Fish giggled with joy, rolling their eyes.

The sun in a tutu, doing a jig,
While waves clapped their hands, the night was big.
We cheered with delight, drinks spilling around,
This boat party was the best ever found!

With laughter and joy, we sailed the vast joy,
In a world of whimsy, like a child with a toy.
As night drew its curtain, we raised a cheer,
For adventures ahead, with no trace of fear.

A Canvas of Fiery Hues

The sky painted orange, what a divine sight,
Like cotton candy spun with sheer delight.
We forgot our maps, oh but that's just fine,
Who needs a compass when the drinks are divine?

The sun wore sunglasses, striking a pose,
While waves ran up laughing, tickling toes.
With every splash, we grinned ear to ear,
And the rubber duck mascot declared "Let's go cheer!"

We perfected our cannonballs, a splashing affair,
While dolphins darted, just to compare.
Their giggles resounded, a playful song,
In a world so absurd, how could we go wrong?

As the vibrant colors faded, we stayed in our groove,
With stories of nonsense, our silly dance moves.
Under a big moon, we knew we were blessed,
In this canvas of laughter, we were always the best!

Lost in the Azure Calm

In waters so blue, we lost track of time,
With snacks on the deck, oh how they did rhyme!
The sandwiches danced like stars in the night,
While our drinks played tag, such a whimsical sight.

A fish caught my eye, it winked with a grin,
As if to say, "Come join in the fin!"
We tried to keep up, but fell in the sea,
Floating like noodles, just bursting with glee.

A frosty breeze chilled, but we were all warm,
With laughter and pranks, it was pure charm.
We played peekaboo with the clouds overhead,
While the moon cracked jokes, tickling us in bed.

What a splendid mess! Our crew's quite the crew,
Drifting through nonsense, all shiny and new.
With each wave that splashed, we danced with the tide,
Lost in the calm, what a jubilant ride!

The Evening's Serenade

The stars began twinkling, like eyes full of cheer,
While fish donned tuxedos, waltzing near.
The moon was a bard, strumming songs on a string,
With laughter and joy, we danced in a fling.

Our boat turned a stage, the waves were the crowd,
With each silly step, we danced well and loud.
Seagulls cheered on, having quite the fun,
And the crabs did the shimmy, under the sun.

We shared goofy secrets, all drunk on the breeze,
While the night wrapped us up, like warm buttered cheese.

With lanterns a-glow, we tipped our hats high,
For just a few hours, we soared through the sky.

As the evening wore on, laughter filled the night,
In this wacky adventure, everything felt right.
With friends by our side, and the sea as our guide,
We'll treasure this night, with giggles and pride.

Illuminated Waters of Farewell

As the sun dips low, we cheer and shout,
Captain's hat askew, who let that out?
The gulls join in, it's quite the squawk,
On our grand vessel, we dance and talk.

The fish are laughing, floating on by,
Did you see that splash? Look at that sky!
With snacks on the deck, what a fine feast,
Let's share this moment, not just the least.

The waves wave back, a cheeky trick,
We all wear life vests, ain't it slick?
With each hearty laugh, the boat sways too,
Our memories are formed like a wild brew.

So here we float, with our hearts in tow,
This farewell's a party, not a sad show!
As the bright light fades, we'll hold on tight,
For every end brings a new delight!

The Dawn of Evening's Promise

Evening falls, we chart our course,
With popcorn in hand, we feel the force.
The wind sings softly, tickling our nose,
As goofy waves dance in happy throws.

Oh look, what's that? A seal in a tie!
Waving its flipper as it swims by.
With laughter we toast with fizzy drinks,
The horizon blushes as the ocean winks.

Our headlights flicker with playful glee,
While our boat performs as dandy as can be.
And every wave brings a chuckle so bright,
For evening's promise is pure marine light.

So here we are, on the edge of the fun,
As the day slips away, we've hardly begun!
With friends by our side, what more could we seek?
Let's ride the night wave for as long as we peek!

A Dream Boat on Twilight's Lake

On a lake that twinkles like a thousand eyes,
We float on a dream, 'neath the cotton candy skies.
With ducks as our crew, we laugh with delight,
Our oars are just paddles in the soft twilight.

A squirrel in a tux, he takes the lead,
In this grand boat race, there's no need for speed.
With snacks on the side, and giggles galore,
We're kings of the water, what fun to explore!

The ripples are laughing, can you hear their cheer?
As we fish for our dreams, they're swimming near.
With the stars as our guide, what a glorious ride,
In this whimsical boat, where imaginations collide.

So let's sail on laughter, let's drift into bliss,
This twilight adventure, you wouldn't want to miss!
With a wink and a grin, our hearts in a fray,
In this dream boat, forever we'll play!

Serene Passage Into Nightfall

As nightfall whispers, the water smiles wide,
With a wink from the moon, on this thrilling ride.
Our boat is a stage, what a comical sight,
As we juggle and dance, under twinkling light.

The stars shine bright, with a wink and a jest,
While the frogs do a chorus, what a silly quest!
With fireflies buzzing like a playful choir,
We tiptoe on waves, as we laugh and inspire.

"Oh no, here come pirates!" we tease with a grin,
But they're just our friends in a boat made of tin.
Sailing around in circles, making a splash,
With each silly caper, we're having a bash.

So we toast to the night, with cupcakes to share,
In our merry escapade, with naught a care.
In this serene passage, let's hold on tight,
For this joyful journey thrives in the night!

Winds of a Dusk-tinted Journey

With laughter in the salty air,
Our ship's crew is quite a pair.
One's seasick, spilling his stew,
While seagulls laugh and join the queue.

The sun's a giant disco ball,
As we attempt our grand sail haul.
With sails all flapping, what a sight,
We'll dance till stars come out at night.

Our compass spins, it's quite a game,
To find our way, it's all the same.
We'll ride the waves, oh what a ride,
With rubber ducks all by our side!

Oh, the horizon paints us bold,
As we ditch maps, brave and uncontrolled.
With giggles and joy, we won't relent,
On this wild voyage, we're heaven-sent.

The Last Flicker of Daylight

As twilight paints the world in hues,
I ponder why I wore these shoes.
They're not meant for this bumpy ride,
Yet here I am, all full of pride.

The sun prepares its soft goodbye,
While fish below just laugh and sigh.
What's that up ahead? A big blue whale?
Or just my mate's ballooning tail?

We toast with soda, what a cheer!
Just me and my crew, full of beer.
The sunset's wild, and so are we,
With laughter echoing o'er the sea.

As stars emerge, we dance a jig,
While our boat does the silliest wig.
With giggles and splashes, we'll forever play,
In the last flicker of this silly day.

A Farewell to the Golden Glow

The sun's a candied lemon drop,
As we prepare for our fun swap.
I left my map, but who needs that?
We'll just follow the dancing cat!

With laughter rising with the tide,
We ride the waves, oh what a ride!
But wait, where's our captain gone?
He's chatting with a parrot, drawn!

As the horizon blushes bright,
Our boat does twirls, quite the sight.
The stars peek out, oh what a tease,
While jellyfish float like they're at ease.

So here's to the glow, as we depart,
With silly smiles and half a heart.
To memories made, we'll laugh and sway,
Farewell to gold, we're on our way!

Shadows on the Water's Surface

The waves reflect our silly stunts,
While shadows dance, avoiding hunts.
Our boat's a tub, we swim and play,
As dolphins lead the wacky way.

The sun bows low, a comic show,
While we're busy trying to row.
With noodles swirling, quite the mess,
We'll chart our course with fun, no stress!

A frog jumps high, what's that? A splash!
Our crew erupts in giggles, a rash.
We wave at fish as they swim by,
Wondering why they don't ask why!

In shadows cast by the setting ray,
We find our joy in everyday play.
With painted skies and hearts of gold,
Our tales are woven, bold yet untold.

The Sea's Lullaby at Dusk

The boat's rocking like a lullaby,
A seagull thinks he's oh so sly.
I tossed him chips with all my might,
And he just laughed, what a silly sight!

The sky's a canvas, colors collide,
Mermaids playing hide and seek, they hide.
I call to them, they giggle and flee,
This journey's a dream, or is it just me?

A fish jumps up, takes a bow,
I whisper, "Is there a talent show now?"
The waves clap back with a cheerful roar,
As I float on by, what's next in store?

With stars appearing, it feels so bold,
Even the moon looks slightly gold.
A dance on the waves, a splash and a spin,
Who knew the sea could be such a win?

A Journey of Dimmed Stars

On a rickety boat, here I sway,
Dueling between fish and salty spray.
Stars are dimming as night calls near,
But I still can't tell if that's a cheer!

A crab waves hello with its little claw,
While flounders dance in a silly draw.
"Join us!" they beckon, "It's quite the show!"
I tumble and trip, oh no! Oh no!

Wind in my hair, and spray on my face,
This watery world, what a wild place!
The sky's now a blanket with twinkling lights,
Pirate dreams fill my mismatched nights.

With each gentle rock, I chuckle out loud,
The ghost of the ocean, I'm feeling quite proud.
What's next, a whale with a top hat and cane?
In this nautical jest, it's all fair game!

Into the Horizon's Gentle Hush

The horizon blushes, a warm yellow glow,
Straight ahead, there's a rubber duck show.
With giggles and bubbles, I can't help but cheer,
This ocean of laughter, so perfectly clear.

"Hold on tight!" I shout to a passing fish,
"Don't miss the boat, it's a funny-wish!"
They flip and they swirl in a dazzling dance,
Maybe this trip is just pure romance!

The wind whispers jokes that only we know,
While clouds parade by in a comical show.
I throw out my line, but what do I catch?
A sock and a spoon! Now that's a great match!

With night creeping in, and stars all aglow,
The sea and I share a secret flow.
What's better than laughter drifting afar?
A boat full of dreams beneath every star!

The Call of Night's Embrace

The ocean's dance is quite the delight,
With jellyfish glowing, a magnificent sight.
I heard one whisper, "Let's float away!"
But I'm stuck with this bucket—where's my pay?

As the sun waves goodbye with a wink,
I spill my drink, oh what a stink!
The fish all giggle, 'Is that what we drink?'
Then they start a wave; I'm on the brink!

Stars twinkle down like they've lost their way,
I ask them to join, come dance and play!
The sea creates giggles, it plays with my heart,
In this twilight adventure, we'll never part.

With each silly wave and splash of foam,
I find my heart in this magical dome.
The call of the night, so funny and free,
Embracing the laughter that lives in the sea!

The Fall of Day's Cloak

As daylight winks and starts to fade,
A boatyard dance, a masquerade.
With fishy hats and a wobbling crew,
They juggle jellyfish, who knew?

Balloons adrift on a salty breeze,
The captain's hat's missing, if you please.
A seagull swoops for his afternoon snack,
And the anchor's tangled in the captain's backpack.

Laughter echoes off the ocean's height,
Each wave a giggle of pure delight.
A splash of color, the sky's last treat,
As we race each other, tripping on our feet.

But as the stars begin their glow,
We chase the tide, oh where'd it go?
For in this blink of twilight's bliss,
We find the sun with a cheeky kiss.

Leaving Footprints in Sunlight

With toes in sand, we set our aim,
On golden trails, a silly game.
We skip and slip, our laughter loud,
While crabs join in, oh so proud.

The sunbeam's snicker, a glowing sly,
As we tumble over, fishy pie.
Each step's a splash, a giggling spree,
"Look, there's a dolphin!"—it's just me!

A picnic basket tips with glee,
As sun hats flitter like bumblebees.
We build a castle, a moat of cheer,
Watch out for waves, they sneak up near!

As shadows stretch, we dance and play,
In this bright and sunny cabaret.
With footprints left like stories spun,
Tomorrow comes, but we'll have our fun.

Threads of Evening Illumination

Like threads unraveled, the light unspools,
Dizzy-heeled dancers, a band of fools.
We twirl in circles, our laughter bright,
With a fish as our guide, it's quite a sight!

The sun dips down, a cheeky grin,
"Let's navigate this chaos, win!"
With map and compass upside down,
The prankster moon dons a twinkly crown.

As shadows play hide and seek,
We fall in heaps, oh what a streak!
Through tangled nets of evening gold,
Exchanging secrets, daring and bold.

So here's to the night, the silly spree,
Where anything goes, just wait and see.
With twinkling stars and a wink from the tide,
We'll ride this wave, come for a ride!

Driftwood Under a Fading Sky

Driftwood dreams on the shifting shore,
While laughter harmonizes, evermore.
A floating boat, a broken oar,
Pirates of silliness, oh what a score!

With upside-down goggles, we spot a whale,
Or is it just Bob, who tells a tall tale?
As snacks go flying with each little wave,
Our treasure hunt's odd, but we're feeling brave.

The sky's a canvas, colors ignite,
Each brushstroke giggles with sheer delight.
As mermaids dance on that choppy foam,
We toss our worries, the ocean's our home.

So here's to driftwood, the tide's sweet tease,
And crabby companions, who giggle with ease.
As the sky darkens, the fun won't cease,
For in the sunset, we find our peace.

The Twilight Odyssey

On a boat that creaks like a door,
With snacks that spill and hit the floor.
We wave at fish as they swim by,
While seagulls laugh, oh my, oh my!

The horizon blushes, a canvas bright,
Our hats fly off like birds in flight.
With every splash, we squeal in glee,
While waves conspiring—such folly!

Echoes of an Embered Sky

With sunburned noses, we race the breeze,
In life jackets bright as yellow peas.
Our captain sneezes, oh what a sight,
As we navigate by pure delight!

The clouds wear shades in a goofy grin,
While fish parade, with scales that spin.
We toast to blunders in goofy cheers,
And laugh at our wet and wobbly fears!

Journeying Through Liquid Gold

Gliding through what seems like soup,
Our boat resembles a floating hoop.
Tides that tickle and waves that chuckle,
We shout, 'Look out!' and huddle in a huddle!

The sun's a giant, dripped in syrup,
While we float by in our delicious cup.
Each splash a comedy, every wave a jest,
Who knew this voyage would be such a fest?

The Tranquil Passage Home

We drift along, the sun ablaze,
With jokes to share for endless days.
A friendly fish joins our silly dance,
While crabs applaud, given the chance!

Home is near, but we're not in haste,
For every laugh is a treasured taste.
With golden hues to warm our hearts,
We're just happy fools, in funny parts!

Navigating Through Amber Waves

In a boat made of cheese, we set sail,
With seagulls who squawk, and they wail.
A fish tried to dance, but fell with a splash,
As we laughed at the waves, they gave quite a crash.

We counted the clouds, one two and three,
They looked like a cat, or maybe a bee.
With ice cream cones stuck to the mast,
We wondered how long this foolishness would last.

Jellyfish twirled, with a wink and a grin,
As we lost track of where our fun began.
The sun winks back at our goofy delight,
For every wrong turn feels startlingly right.

So here's to the fun, on this cheesy ride,
Where laughter and waves go for a wild glide.
We'll dance with the fish and sing with the breeze,
In our floating wonderland, nothing to seize.

Beneath the Blushing Sky

Under a sky blushing bright with hue,
We painted our boat in splashes of blue.
With hats on our heads and sunscreen on nose,
We laughed as the wind tousled hair like a rose.

Our compass spun like a dishwasher's dream,
Directionless drifting became quite the theme.
A crab stole our sandwich, we chased it with glee,
While dolphins laughed, claiming they knew the way to be free.

The sun was a friend, casting shadows so long,
We sang silly songs and got all the words wrong.
With a wink to the stars as the daylight took rest,
Our playful adventure just got a little zest.

As the tide tickled toes, fears began to fade,
And dreams became silly, like a cartwheel parade.
With giggles and splashes, we danced in delight,
Underneath the blushing sky, everything felt right.

Horizon's Serenade

A seagull serenade echoed from afar,
We turned to see where its melodies are.
With a fish on a flute and a crab on a drum,
We knew this adventure would surely be fun!

The horizon waved back, teasing us so,
As we bobbed on the waves, feeling aglow.
With sunglasses askew and hats flying high,
We waved at the pelicans drifting on by.

An octopus joined, strumming our tune,
While jellyfish twirled like they danced to the moon.
Every wave brought a giggle, a splash, and a cheer,
As our funny little boat rolled on without fear.

We closed our eyes, let the rhythm take flight,
With laughter and tales under soft evening light.
Every memory made was a treasure so grand,
In our whimsical world, hand in hand.

The Celestial Mirage

Out on the ocean where the sky meets the sea,
We chased down the seagulls, just as silly as can be.
Caught in a mirage, we ended up lost,
With stars as our compass, we laughed at the cost.

A walrus in sunglasses winked from the shore,
Playing tricks with our minds as we begged him for more.
He juggled some clams while we clapped out of time,
In this riotous dream, we crafted our rhyme.

The sun painted pictures, so absurd but so bright,
With mermaids and pirates joining in on the flight.
We toasted with pineapple drinks made out of foam,
In our boat of lost wonders, we felt so at home.

As the moon tiptoed in on a wave of soft light,
Every chuckle and grin felt exceedingly right.
With jokes like confetti, we sailed through the night,
In the celestial mirage where everything's light.

The Luminous Fade

The boat wobbles, oh what a sight,
As seagulls laugh and take their flight.
With snacks spilling all over the deck,
We chase a wave, what the heck!

The sun dips low, like a sly prank,
While fish below give us a rank.
They flip and splash, trying to tease,
While we just giggle, feeling the breeze.

With drinks in hand and hats askew,
We toast to all that we'll never do.
As light fades fast, we start to glow,
In outfits bright, putting on a show!

The stars peek out, the night takes cue,
While dolphins dance like they just flew.
We laugh and cheer, what a bizarre flight,
As our boat drifts off into the night!

Of Tides and Twilight

The waves decide it's time to play,
While we pretend we know the way.
A cannonball splash, oh what a mess,
As the captain shrieks, 'This is no dress!'

The horizon glows, a funny hue,
While we argue who'll cook the stew.
The fish are watching, they roll their eyes,
As we debate under purple skies.

A pirate hat from who knows where,
A parrot laughs, it seems so rare.
With drinks that wobble, laughter not thin,
Who knew the ocean could spin us in?

Oh twilight brings its giggly charms,
We wave to the audience, in their arms.
With belly laughs, the night begins,
As we forget the day's silly sins!

Horizon-Crossing Reverie

We cast off sails with helter-skelter,
As jellyfish float, what a wonderful melter.
With ice cream cones, we stir the sea,
Trying hard not to spill on me!

The sun is a big yellow pancake,
While fishy friends tease us for our mistake.
We lose a flip-flop, yelling 'oh no!'
As crabs join in, putting on a show.

The seagulls squawk, 'This isn't a race!'
As we paddle about, lost in space.
A sunset snack turns into a feast,
While I blame the waves, my sense has ceased.

Twilight surrounds; the laughter is real,
As we recount tales, oh what a deal!
With stars like sprinkles in the dark sky,
We dream of sailing and giggle nearby.

The Last Voyage of Light

A ship adrift, our caps flown high,
As jellybeans rain from the sky.
With marshmallow clouds below our feet,
We bounce and giggle, can't take the heat!

The sun's a jester, winking away,
As we compete in a game of sway.
With wobbly legs like a newborn deer,
Splashing our drinks, we have no fear!

'Hold tight!' I shout, losing my grip,
As the sea takes us on a wild trip.
With laughter ringing, we spin in delight,
As colors paint the twilight night.

Oh, this last journey, a wild delight,
As whimsy sails on through dusk's light.
Together we float, no worries in sight,
Just friends and good times, our hearts feel light!

Of Stars and Silent Mists

The boat was old, held by quirks,
With sails that flopped like sleepy jerks.
Fish jumped high, like they knew the joke,
As we floated on waves, a gentle poke.

The captain laughed, his hat askew,
While seagulls plotted, a feathery crew.
"Is it just me, or do we smell?"
The ocean replied with a cheery yell.

To spot a star, we searched the sky,
But instead found clouds, all fluffy and shy.
"Is that a comet or just my dinner?"
Laughter erupted, who is the winner?

Finally night fell, the stars were brilliant,
"Anglerfish glow?" the captain was resilient.
Drifting in laughter, we danced with delight,
On this wobbly ride through the canvas of night.

Where the Ocean Meets the Ember

Catch a breeze with a wink and a smirk,
Our boat was a thing that just loved to jerk.
The waves clapped hands, a rhythmic embrace,
As we fumbled around with forgetting our place.

The captain declared, 'It's time to relax!'
And promptly fell off with all of his snacks.
A splash and a giggle, what could go wrong?
We cheered as he floundered, not lasting too long.

With every wave, a new chuckle arose,
While jellyfish danced in their transparent prose.
The sunset chuckled, painting the tide,
While we laughed at the sea, our great turbulence guide.

In the midst of the antics, we somehow found peace,
The ocean's humor never did cease.
As our boat bobbed away, it felt like a dream,
Funny how life flows, just like a stream.

The Radiant Driftwood

Driftwood floated, a high-flying king,
We waved to the dolphins, they did their thing.
The boat squeaked loudly, a crescendo of glee,
"Is that a whale trunk, or just me?"

The wind carried whispers of mates from afar,
While a crab stole our lunch without any spar.
"Ahoy there, crustacean!" we shouted in jest,
As he scuttled away, we're clearly the best.

With surfboards strapped, we dared the swell,
Watching the sunset, we rang the bell.
But the waves like to giggle, and we took a tumble,
In that salty embrace, we couldn't help but mumble.

The colors erupted, oh what a scene,
A joke from the ocean, as vivid as a dream.
Together we floated on this wooden delight,
As laughter echoed and danced through the night.

Sailing in a Painted Sky

We set off for fun in a colorful boat,
With sails that caught sun, oh what a note!
Around us, the sky painted hues like a clown,
As we drifted in laughter and chuckles marked down.

Golden hues splashed, a canvas so bright,
The fish flopped on deck, "Is this dinner tonight?"
Our paddles uncoordinated, an art of their own,
With each squabble and splash, our silliness shone.

Seagulls were laughing, their antics a riot,
Squawking our secrets, we felt quite the diet.
"Who needs a map when you have a boat?"
As our journey became more of a humorous gloat.

When dusk finally whispered, painting things gold,
We toasted to laughter, our joy uncontrolled.
In this painted sky, all was a jest,
With friends by our side, we felt truly blessed.

Reeds and Fading Light

The boat wobbles like a puppy on grass,
As I wave at pelicans who just won't pass.
The wind tells jokes I can barely catch,
While seaweed tickles my toes, what a match!

The horizon blushes, all orange and pink,
I wonder if dolphins stop here to drink.
A crab scuttles by, he's got quite the stride,
If I had his moves, I wouldn't need to glide!

With snacks by my side, I munch and I laugh,
At a seagull who thinks he's the captain of my craft.
Suddenly, I'm the king of the wide, wild sea,
Till my sandwich flies off, oh what a spree!

As the light grows dim, it's an artist's brush,
In a world that makes me giggle in a hush.
Tonight, we'll dance under the fading glow,
With a crew that's all quirks and a hearty row!

An Odyssey to Dusk's Embrace

I set off to chase the horizon with flair,
With a hat blown off by a gust of fresh air.
The stars up above start their playful tease,
While the waves come in giggles, they just won't freeze!

A fish jumps high like he's practicing flight,
He's here for the laughs, what a funny sight.
"Keep it down, fish, I'm trying to think!"
But he just splashes back, spilling my drink!

I spot a lone seagull, regal and proud,
I salute him with laughter, feels good to be loud.
As the colors melt into evening's disguise,
I'm counting the stars and the sass in their eyes!

Under a blanket of twinkling delight,
I fish for memories on this buoyant night.
We'll prank the moon with our silly parade,
And drift into dreams where worries just fade.

Gathering Memories Under the Stars

The sun dips low, with a wink and a grin,
It looks like the day knows where I'd been.
With laughter and maps made in crumpled toast,
We're racing to see who can catch the most!

Crabs join our crew, dressed to impress,
They dance on the beach, oh what a mess!
With buckets of waves and seashells galore,
We're stacking up stories to share and explore!

As twilight blankets our raucous fest,
I tell tales of fish that swim with zest.
They giggle and wiggle with each corny rhyme,
While I chuckle 'til hiccups, oh, what a time!

Under the stars, we weave through our dreams,
While jellyfish glow with our whimsical schemes.
Let's bottle this night, with its laughter and cheer,
And toast to adventures in a world without fear!

The Twilight Canvas

The sky's a palette, all messy and bright,
With brushes of clouds that tickle the night.
I find my boat and give it a kick,
"Let's paint this evening, and hurry, not quick!"

With wobbly waves as my dancing floor,
I try not to spill my drink once more.
The horizon's laughing, my oar's out of sync,
While frogs on the bank croak their own link!

As stars begin popping like popcorn in glee,
I swear I can hear them negotiating with me.
"Just one more joke before the night ends,"
While the moon winks down with all of her friends.

And when I return with tales from the sea,
I'll find all my thoughts wrapped in endless spree.
In colors and giggles, my heart finds its beat,
On this twilight canvas, oh, what a treat!

Twilight's Gilded Horizon

A boat with a parrot, a cap full of flecks,
We laugh at the seagulls stealing our snacks.
The sun winks at us, a cheeky old chap,
As we dodge waves while sharing a map.

With ice cream cones melting, we bumble around,
Our compass points sideways, excitement unbound.
The horizon's aglow, like a disco ball,
We trip on the deck; oh, it's a grand fall!

Our captain's a cat, and he steers us true,
With a feathered hat, he thinks he's so cool.
The dolphins are giggling, they join in the fun,
Waving their tails in the casting sun.

The stars come to play, like confetti in air,
With laughter and music, we float without care.
We dance with the waves, while the night starts to hum,
As the world turns to starlight, oh goodness, we're numb!

The Last Light's Voyage

With ketchup boats sailing on a pickle sea,
We navigate flavors, oh what a spree!
The sun is a giant, all dripping with gold,
As our sandwiches pop up, growing ever bold.

There's a crew of oddballs, a jester and mime,
They jest and they chuckle, turning waves into rhymes.
We hoot with delight at the gulls in tuxedos,
Teaching us dance moves and how to wear speedos.

A treasure map drawn in spaghetti strands,
We dive for the sauce with our curious hands.
Our laughter erupts like a fizz from a drink,
As we splash in the waves, we barely can think.

The moon loves the antics, begins to shine bright,
On a voyage of giggles, we sail through the night.
With a wink and a nod, our wild tales ascend,
It's a buffet of fun, where the laughter won't end!

Journey Beyond the Dusk

A crew of comedians, we set out to roam,
With the wind in our hair, it feels just like home.
The stars are our guides, though a little askew,
We navigate while wearing our mismatched shoe.

The fish are all chuckling, we share in their jest,
As the moon tells us secrets, "You're all quite the pest!"
We argue with shadows, they giggle and play,
In a world full of whimsy, come join our cabaret.

Our sails catch the giggles, the breeze carries cheer,
As jellyfish waltz by, bibbing us near.
With laughter as cannonfire, we conquer the tide,
On this silly adventure, there's nothing to hide.

In twilight's soft glow, we dance with delight,
The horizon's a canvas painted so bright.
As the ocean erupts into dance and into song,
This journey is joyful, our hearts where they belong!

Embracing the Evening Tide

We sprint on the deck with our arms open wide,
As the sunset throws colors, oh what a ride!
Our boat's a wild steed, it hops and it skips,
While we howl like the wind, with plentiful quips.

The crabs do the cha-cha, the clams join the show,
With barnacles clapping, we let our hearts glow.
A floating funhouse, with giggles galore,
As we chat with the fish, craving snacks to explore.

The horizon is silly, it tickles our grins,
As the sky plays its tricks and the giggling begins.
With a splash and a cheer, we embrace the night air,
In the dance of the tides, our troubles lay bare.

As the moon starts to wink, we raise a toast high,
To laughter and joy, to the vast open sky.
In this wonderful journey, we dodge every plight,
With fun as our compass, we sail through the night!

Embers of an Evening Breeze

The ship is wobbling with delight,
My hat flies off—what a sight!
The seagulls mock, they're quite the crew,
Chasing sunsets, like they're in a revue.

Splashing waves with goofy glee,
The captain's lost but drinks his tea.
A fish jumps high, then makes a splash,
My sandwich flies, oh what a crash!

We hoot and holler at the breeze,
With teetering steps, we dance with ease.
The stars remind us it's time to be fun,
As lanterns twinkle, our night's begun.

So here we are, adrift in cheer,
With laughter loud; no hint of fear.
The evening glows, with jokes we tease,
Let's ride the waves, oh take it, please!

Drift Between Day and Night

The sky wears colors quite absurd,
My friend thinks he's a flying bird.
He flaps his arms, a sight to see,
While I just grin, quite happily.

As daylight bids a silly goodbye,
The moon peeks in with a curious eye.
A crab claps claws, a comical sound,
We can't help but tumble all around.

The shadows dance like silly fools,
We're "experts" at breaking all the rules.
Each drift brings laughter in big doses,
While groans escape from tired, sore noses.

With stars above like proud little knights,
We're here to roam, beneath the lights.
Embracing night like a funky game,
No day too wild, no night too tame!

The Horizon's Gentle Caress

We ride the waves on a silly spree,
My pants are drenched, oh woe is me!
The fish are laughing, what a show,
As I splash around, like it's a pro.

The sun waves back, or so I think,
With shades so bright, it gives a wink.
A dolphin leaps; oh, there it goes,
While I struggle with my tippy toes.

We twirl and jig, a quirky sight,
Our boat's a stage dimming with light.
The bobbing rhythm is off the chart,
An evening dance, straight from the heart.

So let's embrace this crazy vibe,
As we sail on out, right past the tribe.
With giggles and cheers, we'll steal the scene,
The horizon's our stage, it's snug and clean!

Secrets Held by Dusk's Veil

Beneath the stars, we plot our scheme,
To create the silliest dream team.
With quirks and laughs, we look for fun,
As night arrives, and day is done.

The breeze whispers secrets, oh so sly,
Swaying us gently, as we float by.
A clownfish waves, he's quite the chap,
While I grab snacks—oh, there's my cap!

The moon grins down, like it knows our jest,
With giggles rising, we're feeling blessed.
A treasure map's drawn with crumbs of bread,
To an island where rumor says we're fed!

So let's keep drifting in this wild play,
All secrets shared in our goofy sway.
With dusk as our friend, we dance till dawn,
In this whimsical world, we carry on!

Whispers of the Dying Day

The boat is wobbly, oh what a sight,
As seagulls laugh, they take their flight.
We spill our drinks, while the sun turns red,
And toast to the waves, not just to the bread.

A fish jumps high, it thinks it's a star,
While we shout, "Hey, that's our dinner, bizarre!"
The captain sneezes, the map goes flying,
As we all wonder, just where are we trying?

Fragments of a Fiery Farewell

The horizon blazes, like grandma's stew,
We wave to the clouds, and they wave back too.
A pirate hat flaps on my pal's head,
While he tries to chant, "We're well really fed!"

With a splash and a giggle, we tip over side,
Giggling like kids, we lose all our pride.
The sun grins at us, on its way to bed,
And we just float on, with fishy dreams in our head.

Charting a Course for Twilight

The compass spins wild, like a merry dance,
While the moon tries on its evening pants.
We're plotting our path with snacks in hand,
And hoping the stars join our frosty band.

Oh look! A dolphin, playing tag with the breeze,
It steals my hat, which it finds a tease!
We laugh till we cry, the night starts to hum,
As we float along, just being, here, dumb.

Where Sky Meets Water's Embrace

The sky is a canvas, painted in hues,
While dancing waves sport a glittery fuse.
We argue 'bout clouds, is it a duck or a bear?
While the fish outsmart us, just floating with flair.

A sunset parade, with fruit punch on deck,
Causing hiccups and giggles, what a wreck!
As we point to the waves, claiming them ours,
And the sunset chuckles, stealing our stars.

Charting Dreams at Dusk

With maps that fold like origami,
We navigate the laughing sea.
Our compass spins in cheeky jest,
A crab waves as we jest and quest.

Balloons float by, tied to our mast,
As seagulls squawk, they fly too fast.
The wind whispers secrets, so absurd,
While fish poke fun at our every word.

Shades of Orange and Indigo

The sky's a painter, with colors bright,
A catfish dons a beret tonight.
Sunset's hue, a slapstick show,
As dolphins dance and steal the glow.

We sip our drinks with tiny umbrellas,
Laughing at rumors of underwater fella.
Chasing hues, we glide and spin,
While octopuses giggle as we begin.

A Fisherman's Farewell

As fish jump high, they bid adieu,
A fisherman waves with a rubber shoe.
His net's tangled—what a grand mess,
With a wink he calls it a 'fishing success!'

The tide pulls strong, a playful tug,
His catch escapes, oh what a shrug!
With laughter echoing in the breeze,
He ponders dinner, or maybe cheese?

The Calm Before Night's Arrival

The boat rocks gently, lulled by the sea,
A playful otter looks back at me.
Stars peek out from their cozy beds,
While a fish splashes—what a full spread!

The lullaby of waves begins to hum,
Tickling my toes, oh, what fun!
With fireflies joining in the night,
The world's a circus, pure delight.

Echoes of a Sunlit Past

A boat on a swing, in the evening's glow,
The captain's at helm, with snacks in tow.
Seagulls are laughing, they steal our fries,
While we toast with sodas, 'neath pink-paint skies.

The waves do a jig, they bubble and bounce,
A fish jumps aboard, and nearly pounces.
We glance at each other, our hats askew,
"Did that fish just wink?" "I think it likes stew!"

The sun starts to dip, in a race with the breeze,
Our jokes grow sillier, quite a tease.
With every wave, our laughter takes flight,
Who needs the horizon, when jokes feel so right!

As night marches in, we spot a tin can,
A treasure from sailors, or just from a man?
In the glow of the moon, with silliness vast,
We'll treasure this trip, and the echoes at last.

A Refuge in the Radiant Skies

A floating affair, on this silly boat ride,
With oversized hats and a cooler beside.
The sun's shining bright, but the captain's all wet,
He thought waves were friends, but they're not, I bet!

Cracking up laughter, as we roll with the tide,
Our sunburned noses, a badge of our pride.
"Ocean, be gentle!" we holler and yell,
While fish stick their heads up, wave, and then dwell.

The sky hints of orange, like orange juice spills,
And a dolphin pops up, it's got some skills.
"Dance with me, buddy!" I shout in the fun,
But it flips with a splash, and says, "Yeah, I'm done!"

With sun on our backs and smiles in our sights,
We drift with the waves like pirate delights.
As stars start to twinkle, our ship's now a star,
In our merry boat dream, we've come oh so far!

The Solstice of Stillness

A gentle bobbing, as the day waves goodbye,
Our boat's quite the wobbler, oh my, oh my!
The sun's lazy blush drapes over our snacks,
"Oh look!" shouts a friend, "there's a fish in slacks!"

The horizon's a canvas, twinkling so bright,
We're painting our questions with laughter and light.
"Is that a boat anchor, or sea monster's glue?"
"Just hold on tight, lest it eats me and you!"

The horizon is rosy, as we swap our tall tales,
Imagining treasures from faraway trails.
With seaweed as crowns, we honor our reign,
This kingdom of humor, in silliness we'll claim.

As the twilight creeps in, we toast to our fun,
Each wave is a laugh, we're all truly one.
With giggles and chuckles as our nighttime song,
We bob in the calm, where we all belong.

When Daylight Meets the Ocean

With pizza on deck, and drinks on the way,
We're a fleet of fools at the end of the day.
The sun starts to droop, like a sleepy old head,
Telling the ocean, "I'm off to my bed!"

We catch ourselves giggling, the wind in our hair,
As seagulls debate who's the king of the air.
"Watch out for the waves, they're feisty and bold!"
But fish just chuckle, their stories retold.

As twilight approaches, it's time for a toast,
To the boat that we claim, and the jokes we love most.
With every wave's giggle, and each splash that we see,
We'll laugh till we're hoarse, oh so blissfully free!

So here's to the sunsets, and silly old days,
The ocean's our stage, as we dance and we sway.
With laughter so hearty, we drop anchor low,
In this whimsical ride, let the good times flow!

A Quiet Sojourn Over the Sea

The boat did bob like a tiny cork,
While seagulls squawked at the lonely dork.
Captain's hat flew, a comical sight,
As waves stole laughs in the fading light.

Fish jumped up, just to tease our snacks,
Snickers arose from my dancing acts.
With a splash, they dived in a fray,
Leaving me asking, 'Who needs a buffet?'

A jellyfish floated, glowing and bright,
It winked at me with a starry delight.
I offered it lunch, a roll and some jam,
But it simply shrugged and went on its scam.

So we drift in giggles, no cares on the mast,
Counting silly seagulls, each one a blast.
On a sea so wide, with laughter in tow,
Who knew the ocean was such a show!

The Whisper of Evening's Breath

The breeze tickled noses, a cheeky tease,
As we watched the sails dance with the ease.
Another fish caught, but it laughed and swam,
Leaving us puzzled; 'Was that a prank, man?'

Stars blinked above like they're winking at me,
While dolphins donned shades, so cool, so free.
Cracked jokes with a whale, he's a hit at the bar,
Said, 'Why don't you join? We'll take it too far!'

An octopus juggled, eight arms in the air,
With jellybean hats to spread laughter and flair.
I wanted to join, but my juggling's a flop,
So I danced with the squids, until they said 'Stop!'

Yet with every giggle, the horizon grew red,
The sun whispered secrets, 'It's time for bed.'
But with all this fun, who wants to depart?
We'll sail 'til we tire, with laughter to chart!

Resplendent Waters Beneath Starlight

Under bright stars, the octopus pranced,
While fish in tuxedos seemed quite entranced.
Crickets chirped tales of a pirate's lost loot,
But we laughed so hard, we fell off the boot!

The dinghy tipped over, splashing us all,
Each member aboard found themselves in a sprawl.
They splashed and they squealed, like kids in a pool,
While I, being clever, just played the cool fool.

As the moon cast her glow, a spotlight above,
A narwhal appeared, like it just fell in love.
It sang a sweet tune, all sparkly and sly,
And we couldn't help laughing, oh my, oh my!

With laughter like bubbles, we floated with glee,
In a world of whimsy, just you and me.
So raise up your glass, let's toast to the night,
For under the stars, we soar with delight!

Cadence of the Last Light

As the sun dripped down, a splash of bright gold,
Our boat rocked gently, with stories retold.
We danced on the deck, under skies turning pink,
Just a crew full of misfits, too silly to think.

The fish were our audience, they gave us a cheer,
With bubbles like laughter, oh what a fun sphere!
A crab in a bowtie, tipped its hat with a grin,
Claimed it was off to join in for a win!

Each wave brought a chuckle, each gust a good laugh,
While gulls cawed their jokes, incomprehensible chaff.
But we shared all the humor, no moment went to waste,
As we floated on whimsy, with glee to embrace.

Now the end of this journey, with shadows now cast,
We say, 'What a trip! Let's just make it last!'
For memories linger beneath the night's hue,
In our hearts still dancing, just me and you.

Embracing the Twilight Waves

The yacht is wobbling like a jelly bean,
My friends are dancing, you should have seen!
With ice cream cones and sunburned noses,
We're laughing hard as the sunset dozes.

The seagulls squawk, they want our fries,
They dive and swoop, oh, what a surprise!
Our captain's hat is two sizes too big,
But that doesn't stop us from doing a jig.

The lighthouse blinks a quirky rhythm,
We can't keep still, it's serious schism.
With waves that toss and a breeze that laughs,
We draw mustaches on our photographs!

As the horizon turns a cheeky shade,
We're yelling jokes, not afraid to parade.
With every splash and every fun pun,
We embrace the twilight, oh, what a run!

Journey to the Dying Day

Buckets of popcorn on the cabin floor,
Our snacks are rolling, oh what a chore!
The sun dips low, like a tired cat,
Winking at us, saying 'How about that?'

With shouts of glee, the crew's on fire,
We might just start a snack attack choir!
Our sunscreen glistens like crazy glue,
Making us stick together, how rude!

The ship's bell dings with a silly clang,
While I'm wearing a pink flamingo tang.
A wave crashes as my drink does too,
The ocean's giggling, it's joining our crew!

We're riding waves with our cheerful flair,
And now I have seaweed tangled in my hair!
The dying day waves a goofy goodbye,
As we turn to shore, with dreams to fly!

Whispers of the Golden Skies

The sunbeams wink like they're in on the joke,
While salty breezes make our sails poke.
We're high-fiving dolphins, they join our parade,
In this funny moment we've all made.

The horizon blushes, oh look at that hue!
We're wearing sunglasses to check out the view.
A parrot squawks, "Where's the party at?"
We toss it a sandwich, called it a spat!

With laughter echoing, we chart our course,
Through golden whispers, we ride the force.
The horizon teases, with lines that are funny,
Waving us on like it's all just honey!

Fishes leap, showing their shiny scales,
We cheer them on, like they're telling tales.
The golden skies soon kiss the water's edge,
And we're still giggling, like a fun pledge!

Anchored in Evening's Glow

The boat has settled, we're anchored tight,
With snacks in hand, we're ready for night.
The stars peek out, pulling a prank,
As we sip our drinks from a rubber plant!

The captain's dancing with a rubber duck,
While we all cheer, "Well, won't this suck?"
With ticklish waves that make us all shake,
We laugh till we cry, for goodness' sake!

As the moon's glow sprinkles all over the tide,
We share funny stories, no reason to hide.
The evening whispers, it knows how to tease,
With every wave, we're trying to please!

The laughter echoes, a chorus so bright,
In the glow of the evening, all feels just right.
As we drop our anchors and float in this show,
We capture the night, anchored in glow!